D1377190

Know Your Quarry

Annie Wendt Hemstock

PowerKiDS
press.
New York

Published in 2015 by The Rosen Publishing Group, Inc.
29 East 21st Street, New York, NY 10010

First Edition

Editor: Amelie von Zumbusch
Book Design: Greg Tucker
Book Layout: Joe Carney
Photo Research: Katie Stryker

Photo Credits: Cover RubberBall Productions/Vetta/Getty Images; pp. 4, 6, 10 Tom Reichner/Shutterstock.com; p. 5 Peter J. Anderson - Seattle/Moment/Getty Images; p. 7 Brent Paull/iStock/Thinkstock; p. 8 aspen rock/Shutterstock.com; p. 9 Domenic Gareri /Shutterstock.com; pp. 11, 29 Fuse/Thinkstock; p. 12 Emi/Shutterstock.com; p. 13 Bildagentur Zoonar GmbH/Shutterstock.com; p. 15 Lois McCleary/Shutterstock.com; p. 17 Phillip W. Kirkland/Shutterstock.com; p. 18 ironman100/iStock/Thinkstock; p. 19 Design Pics/Thinkstock; p. 20 justinecottonphotography/iStock/Thinkstock; p. 21 Fuse /Getty Images; p. 22 eans/Shutterstock.com; p. 23 Marcel Jancovic/Shutterstock.com; p. 25 Stephen Gorman/Aurora/Getty Images; p. 26 KennStilger47/Shutterstock.com; p. 27 Steve Oehlenschlager/Shutterstock.com.

Library of Congress Cataloging-in-Publication Data

Hemstock, Annie Wendt, author.
  Know your quarry / by Annie Wendt Hemstock. — First edition.
     pages cm. — (Open season)
  Includes index.
  ISBN 978-1-4777-6720-7 (library binding) — ISBN 978-1-4777-6721-4 (pbk.) —
  ISBN 978-1-4777-6722-1 (6-pack)
  1. Hunting—Juvenile literature. 2. Game and game-birds—Juvenile literature. I. Title.
  SK35.5.H385 2015
  799.2—dc23
                                        2014002357

Manufactured in the United States of America

CPSIA Compliance Information: Batch #WS14PK3: For Further Information contact Rosen Publishing, New York, New York at 1-800-237-9932

Contents

People have hunted for thousands of years. The kinds of animals we hunt are called game. A single animal that we hunt is our quarry.

It is important to know about the animal you are hunting. Where the animal lives is its **habitat**. Good habitat has food, water, and **cover**. Learning about the habitat for each **species** will help you pick the best hunting areas.

The white-tailed deer is the favorite quarry of many hunters. It is hunted in many parts of the United States.

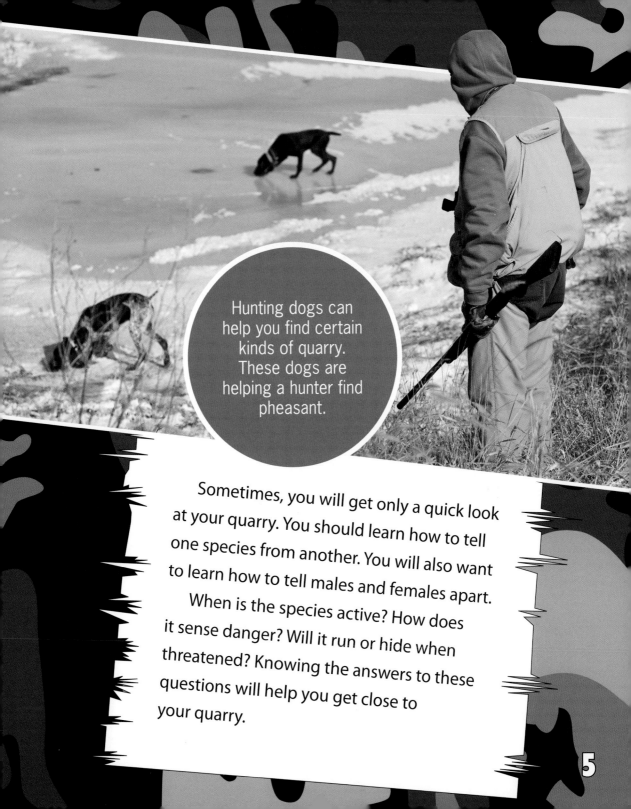

Hunting dogs can help you find certain kinds of quarry. These dogs are helping a hunter find pheasant.

Sometimes, you will get only a quick look at your quarry. You should learn how to tell one species from another. You will also want to learn how to tell males and females apart. When is the species active? How does it sense danger? Will it run or hide when threatened? Knowing the answers to these questions will help you get close to your quarry.

Deer, elk, and moose are big-game animals. They are all members of the deer family. Mule deer live only in western North America. White-tailed deer live in most parts of North America, with the exception of Alaska, northern Canada, and the southwestern United States. Elk live in forests, mainly in the West. Moose live in the Rocky Mountains, Canada, and northern states such as Maine and Minnesota.

Male moose can weigh as much as 1,600 pounds (726 kg). They are also known as bull moose. They are definitely big game!

Hunting Facts

Stands are platforms above the ground, often in trees. A blind is something you sit inside to stay hidden. Stands and blinds help keep your quarry from spotting you.

Bears are also big-game animals. North America is home to three kinds of bears. They are the black bear, the polar bear, and the brown bear, seen here.

Many animals use their ears and nose to warn them of danger. Learn to use the wind to keep your quarry from hearing or smelling you. Many hunters use a tree stand or blind. Knowing about the animals you hunt will help you know where to put one. It will also help you learn the best time to use it.

Because of their size, small-game animals are harder to spot. Many are active at night or are good at hiding. Rabbits can sit very still, hoping you will not see them. If you stop walking and wait, they might leave their hiding spots. Gray squirrels are most active the first few hours after sunrise. Do you know the sounds they make? Listening carefully can help you locate them.

Eastern fox squirrels live in the South and Midwest. They are the largest kind of tree squirrel, usually measuring between 10 and 15 inches (25–38 cm) long.

Raccoons have five toes, just as people do. Their paws are very sensitive. They often wash their food in water because water makes their paws even more sensitive.

Many small-game hunters use dogs to find game. Raccoons will often hide in trees if dogs or hunters get too close. Rabbits will often circle back when dogs chase them. Take time to learn about your quarry. The more you know about their habits, the more successful you can be.

Ducks and geese are waterfowl. They can be a challenge to hunt. The birds have to feel safe to fly close to where hunters are waiting. To keep the birds from seeing them, hunters often use blinds. When you know your quarry, you will know the best place to set up your blind.

Many waterfowl hunters avoid shooting ducks that are in the water. They will shoot only waterfowl that are in flight, as these northern pintails are.

Hunting Facts

Learn to tell different species of waterfowl apart. Note any patches of color, body size, and shape. Watch how they fly, alone and in a flock.

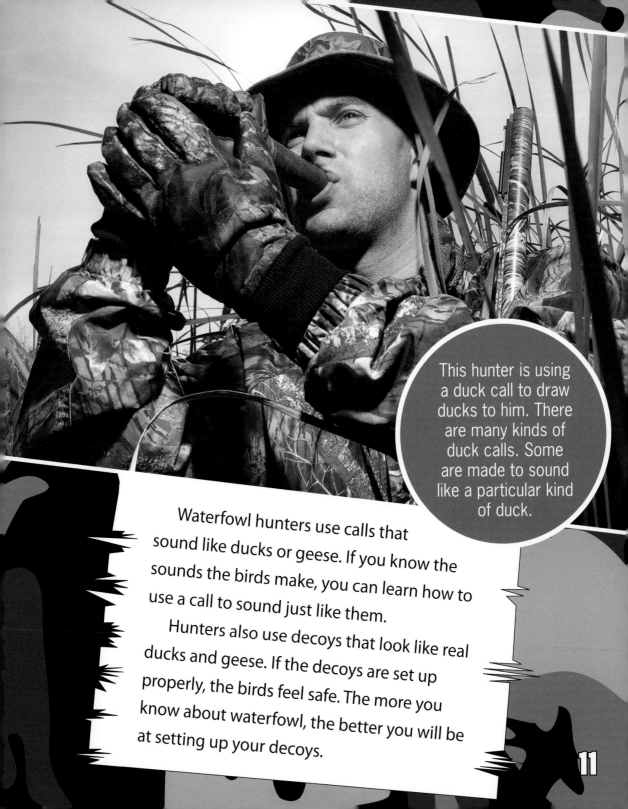

This hunter is using a duck call to draw ducks to him. There are many kinds of duck calls. Some are made to sound like a particular kind of duck.

Waterfowl hunters use calls that sound like ducks or geese. If you know the sounds the birds make, you can learn how to use a call to sound just like them.

Hunters also use decoys that look like real ducks and geese. If the decoys are set up properly, the birds feel safe. The more you know about waterfowl, the better you will be at setting up your decoys.

Knowing Game Birds

There are many species of game birds. Grouse, pheasant, and quail are all upland game. Some game birds, like ruffed grouse, live in forests. Others, like pheasant, live in open country.

Learning about your quarry's habitat will help you find good places to hunt. Does the animal use parts of its habitat at certain times? Does it travel to feeding areas a certain way? Knowing how an animal uses its habitat will help narrow your search.

Gambel's quail live in the deserts of the American Southwest. When looking for them, remember that they generally live near water and often hide in mesquite thickets.

Pheasant are most often found in open fields. These colorful birds are not native to North America. They were introduced from Asia in the late nineteenth century.

The colors and patterns of a bird's feathers act as **camouflage**. Game birds are also very good at hiding, so they are hard to spot. Many hunters will use trained dogs for hunting game birds. Knowing your quarry's habits will help you figure out the best way to hunt them.

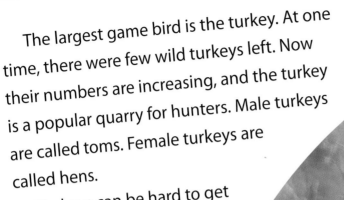

The largest game bird is the turkey. At one time, there were few wild turkeys left. Now their numbers are increasing, and the turkey is a popular quarry for hunters. Male turkeys are called toms. Female turkeys are called hens.

Turkeys can be hard to get close to because they are very **wary**. They can see and hear very well. Hunters use camouflage clothing or blinds to keep from being spotted.

Early morning is one of the best times to find wild turkeys. That is when flocks of the birds look for food in forest clearings and along the edges of fields and roads.

Toms will gobble and **strut** to impress the hens. They compete with other toms for mates. Hunters can use turkey decoys to lure the toms close. They also use calls that sound like gobbling toms or clucking hens. When you know how turkeys act, you can use that information to help you hunt them.

Where does your quarry go to find food? Where is the closest water for it to drink? Where will it go to find a safe place to rest? All animals need food, water, and cover.

Most hunters spend time in the areas they hunt when it is not hunting season. They look for signs that animals have been there. They look for trails to and from food or water. They watch to see where the animals spend different parts of the day. This is called scouting.

If you know the area in which you are hunting, it is a lot easier to figure out where to look for quarry. You are also much less likely to get lost.

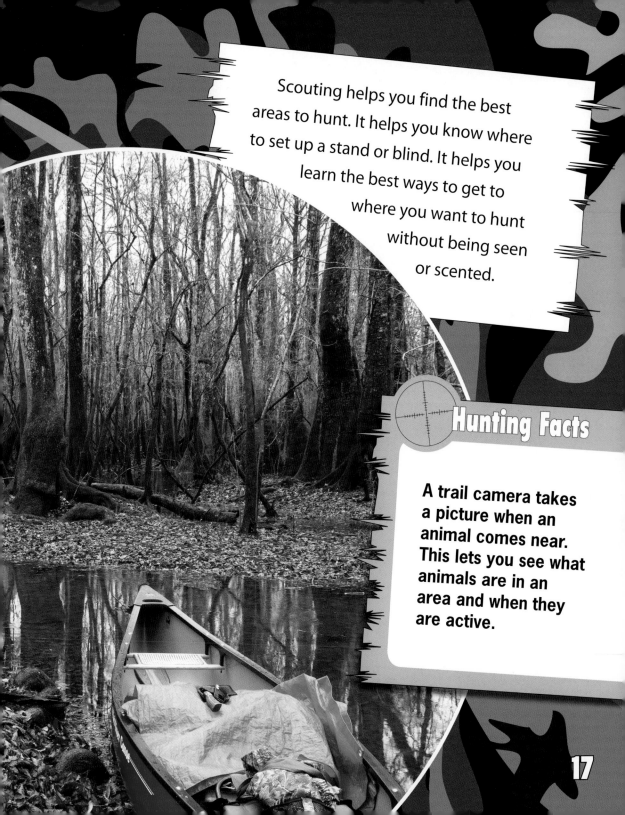

Scouting helps you find the best areas to hunt. It helps you know where to set up a stand or blind. It helps you learn the best ways to get to where you want to hunt without being seen or scented.

Hunting Facts

A trail camera takes a picture when an animal comes near. This lets you see what animals are in an area and when they are active.

Tracking is a very useful skill for hunters. To track an animal, you have to know the kinds of signs it leaves behind. These signs are called **spoor**. Footprints, or tracks, are the most common kind of spoor. Do you know what your quarry's tracks look like? Does it have a hoof? How many toe pads does it have on its front feet and back feet? Do the claws leave marks when it walks?

Deer often keep reusing the same route to reach food and water sources. Be on the lookout for the paths that their movement creates.

18

These are wolf tracks. Wolf tracks look a lot like coyote, fox, and dog tracks. However, wolf tracks are much bigger than those tracks are.

How big are the tracks? The size can let you know if you are following a deer or an elk. Size is also a clue as to whether you are looking at a coyote track or a fox track. With practice, some trackers can even tell one deer from another deer by looking at the tracks.

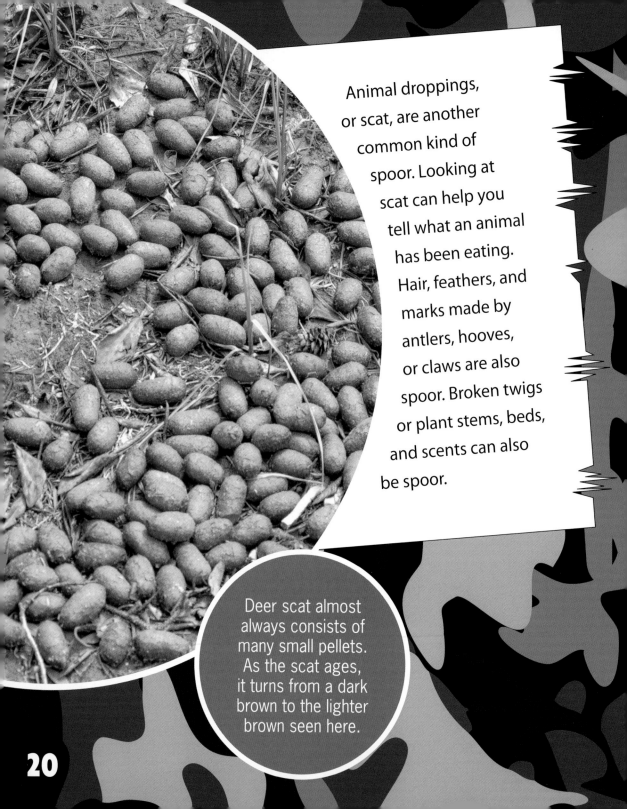

Animal droppings, or scat, are another common kind of spoor. Looking at scat can help you tell what an animal has been eating. Hair, feathers, and marks made by antlers, hooves, or claws are also spoor. Broken twigs or plant stems, beds, and scents can also be spoor.

Deer scat almost always consists of many small pellets. As the scat ages, it turns from a dark brown to the lighter brown seen here.

Becoming a good tracker takes time. You can learn a lot of great tracking tips by talking to a more experienced hunter.

The more you know about your quarry, the easier it will be to follow the spoor. The more you practice tracking, the better you will become. Learning to be a good tracker will help you be a better hunter. Tracking will help you find quarry to hunt. It will also help you find an animal you have hit. Good hunters always track injured game until they find the animal or there is no more sign to follow.

Choose Your Weapon

Most hunters use rifles or shotguns. Some people would rather hunt with bows. It is important to choose the right weapon.

Shotguns shoot many small pellets that spread out when they leave the gun. They work well for hunting birds and small, moving game that are close. A rifle shoots a single bullet that can travel a long distance. Rifles work well for hunting animals that are farther away.

This hunter is using a rifle to hunt moose. Rifles are a good choice for hunting these large animals.

Hunting Facts

Make sure your ammunition is made for your gun. The barrel is marked to tell you what kind to buy. There are also charts to help match the ammunition to your quarry.

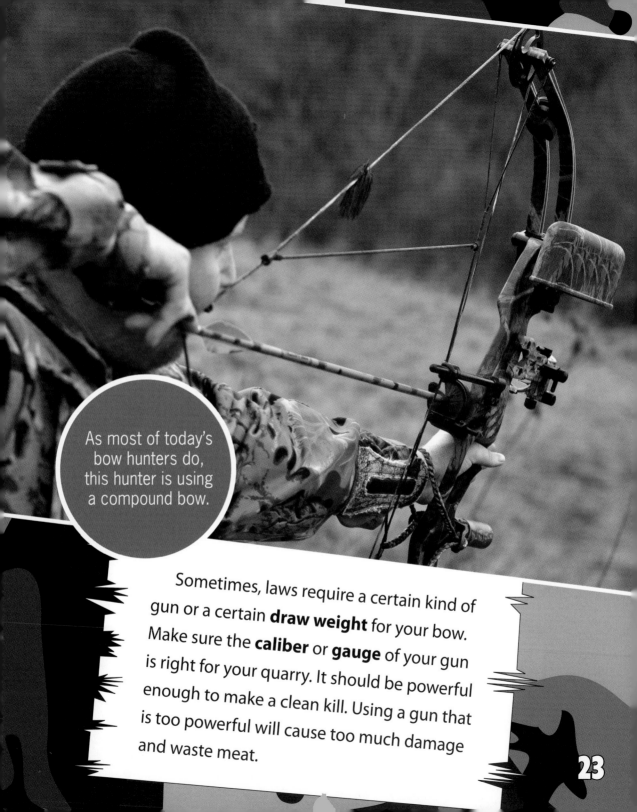

As most of today's bow hunters do, this hunter is using a compound bow.

Sometimes, laws require a certain kind of gun or a certain **draw weight** for your bow. Make sure the **caliber** or **gauge** of your gun is right for your quarry. It should be powerful enough to make a clean kill. Using a gun that is too powerful will cause too much damage and waste meat.

Know the Laws

There are many laws that hunters should know and obey. You may need to have a **license**. You may need to take a class about hunter safety. Sometimes, you have to use a certain kind of gun or wear a certain kind of clothes. You may to need register your kill or treat your quarry in a certain way.

The part of the year when you can hunt is the hunting season. It can be different if you hunt with a bow rather than a gun. It can be different for each kind of animal. The number of animals of a species you can legally take is the bag limit. It is your job to know the laws before you go out hunting.

New Hampshire, where this man is hunting, requires waterfowl hunters to buy a federal duck stamp, a New Hampshire migratory waterfowl license, and a New Hampshire hunting license.

Good hunters know that it is important to obey hunting laws. Some animals are **scarce** because we have changed their habitats. Others were hunted until there were not many left. Today, there are laws to make sure that animal **populations** stay healthy.

For some species, you can hunt only males. There may be laws about how big antlers have to be. Some animals cannot be hunted at all. These kinds of laws ensure that enough animals survive each year.

In many places, there are two turkey-hunting seasons. In the spring, only toms can be hunted. In the fall, it is legal to hunt either toms or hens.

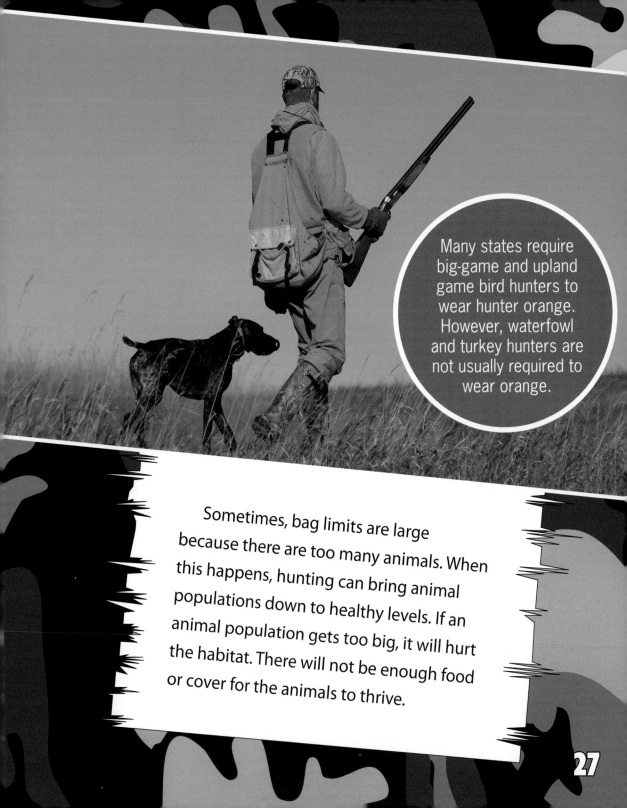

Many states require big-game and upland game bird hunters to wear hunter orange. However, waterfowl and turkey hunters are not usually required to wear orange.

Sometimes, bag limits are large because there are too many animals. When this happens, hunting can bring animal populations down to healthy levels. If an animal population gets too big, it will hurt the habitat. There will not be enough food or cover for the animals to thrive.

People choose to hunt for different reasons. Many enjoy the challenge. Others like to spend time outdoors. Some hunters want to provide meat for their family without buying it at the store.

When you learn about your quarry, you learn about more than just that animal. You learn about where it lives, whether it is the woods, the marsh, or the desert. You learn about the plants that grow there. You learn about other animals that share its habitat. You see how living things depend on each other.

Many hunters enjoy the fact that hunting gives them a chance to spend time outside with friends and family members who also hunt.

You learn how to blend in so you will not be seen. You learn how to keep quiet so you will not be heard. When you hunt, you are part of the natural world.

29

Happy Hunting

- ⊕ Be familiar with how your gun or bow works.

- ⊕ Practice until you can hit where you aim. A good hunter should be a good shot.

- ⊕ Take care of your hunting equipment so it will work properly.

- ⊕ Choose the right ammunition or arrowhead for your quarry. There are charts to help you pick the right kind.

- ⊕ Always use a safety harness when hunting from a tree stand.

- ⊕ Never point your gun or bow at something you do not plan to shoot.

- ⊕ Know what is in front of and behind your target before you take a shot.

- ⊕ Be aware of other hunters nearby.

- ⊕ Be sure of your target. Do not assume that what you saw or heard is your quarry. It may be another hunter.

- ⊕ Keep your finger away from the trigger until you are ready to shoot.

- ⊕ Know and obey the hunting laws for your area.

Glossary

caliber (KA-luh-ber) A measurement of how wide a gun's opening is.

camouflage (KA-muh-flahj) A pattern that matches its surroundings.

cover (KUH-ver) Something that supplies natural shelter for an animal.

draw weight (DRAW WAYT) The amount of force needed to draw a bow in order to shoot an arrow.

gauge (GAYJ) A measure of how wide the barrel of a gun is.

habitat (HA-buh-tat) The kind of land where an animal or a plant naturally lives.

license (LY-suns) Official permission to do something.

populations (pop-yoo-LAY-shunz) Groups of animals or people living in the same place.

scarce (SKERS) Small in amount, hard to find, and often wanted very much.

species (SPEE-sheez) A single kind of living thing. All people are one species.

spoor (SPUHR) Signs that wild animals have been in a place.

strut (STRUT) To walk in a proud manner.

wary (WER-ee) Careful and on the watch for danger.

Index

Websites

Due to the changing nature of Internet links, PowerKids Press has developed an online list of websites related to the subject of this book. This site is updated regularly. Please use this link to access the list: www.powerkidslinks.com/os/know/